EXPLORING SPACE

PLANETS

WRITTEN BY E.C. ANDREWS

Gareth Stevens PUBLISHING

Please visit our website, www.garethstevens.com. For a free color catalog of all our high-quality books, call toll free 1-800-542-2595 or fax 1-877-542-2596.

Published in 2025 by
Gareth Stevens Publishing
2544 Clinton St.
Buffalo, NY 14224

Written by:
E.C. Andrews

Edited by:
Noah Leatherland

Designed by:
Ker Ker Lee

Cataloging-in-Publication Data

Names: Andrews, E.C.
Title: Planets / E.C. Andrews.
Description: Buffalo, NY : Gareth Stevens Publishing, 2025. | Series: Exploring space | Includes glossary and index.
Identifiers: ISBN 9781482468663 (pbk.) | ISBN 9781482468670 (library bound) | ISBN 9781482468687 (ebook)
Subjects: LCSH: Planets--Juvenile literature.
Classification: LCC QB602.A537 2025 | DDC 523.4--dc23

Printed in the United States of America

CPSIA compliance information: Batch #CW25GS: For further information contact Gareth Stevens at 1-800-542-2595.

Find us on

Photo Credits – Images are courtesy of Shutterstock.com. With thanks to Getty Images, Thinkstock Photo and iStockphoto.

Recurring images – Vector Tradition. Cover – Vadim Sadovski. 2–3 – Elena11. 4–5 – Triff, Christos Georghiou. 6–7 – 24K-Production, buradaki, Gilmanshini. 8–9 – NASA images, Gilmanshin, Artsiom P. 10–11 – D-VISIONS, UrbanArtr. 12–13 – Alones, Artsiom P, itechno. 14–15 – Vadim Sadovski, GizemG, M-SUR, M-SUR. 16–17 – Vadim Sadovski Giorces, CC BY 2.5 <https://creativecommons.org/licenses/by/2.5>, via Wikimedia Commons, Kevin M. Gill, CC BY 2.0 <https://creativecommons.org/licenses/by/2.0>, via Wikimedia Commons. 18–19 – buradaki. 20–21 – carlosramos1946, Artsiom P, Andrij Vatsyk. 22–23 – Anterovium, NASA images.

CONTENTS

Words that look like this can be found in the glossary on page 24.

WHAT IS SPACE?

Space is the home of our solar system. Space is the huge area outside of Earth. Many scientists think space is infinite, meaning it goes on forever. However, nobody knows this for sure.

A planet is something in space that orbits around a star. In our solar system, every planet orbits a star called the sun. Earth is just one of eight planets in our solar system.

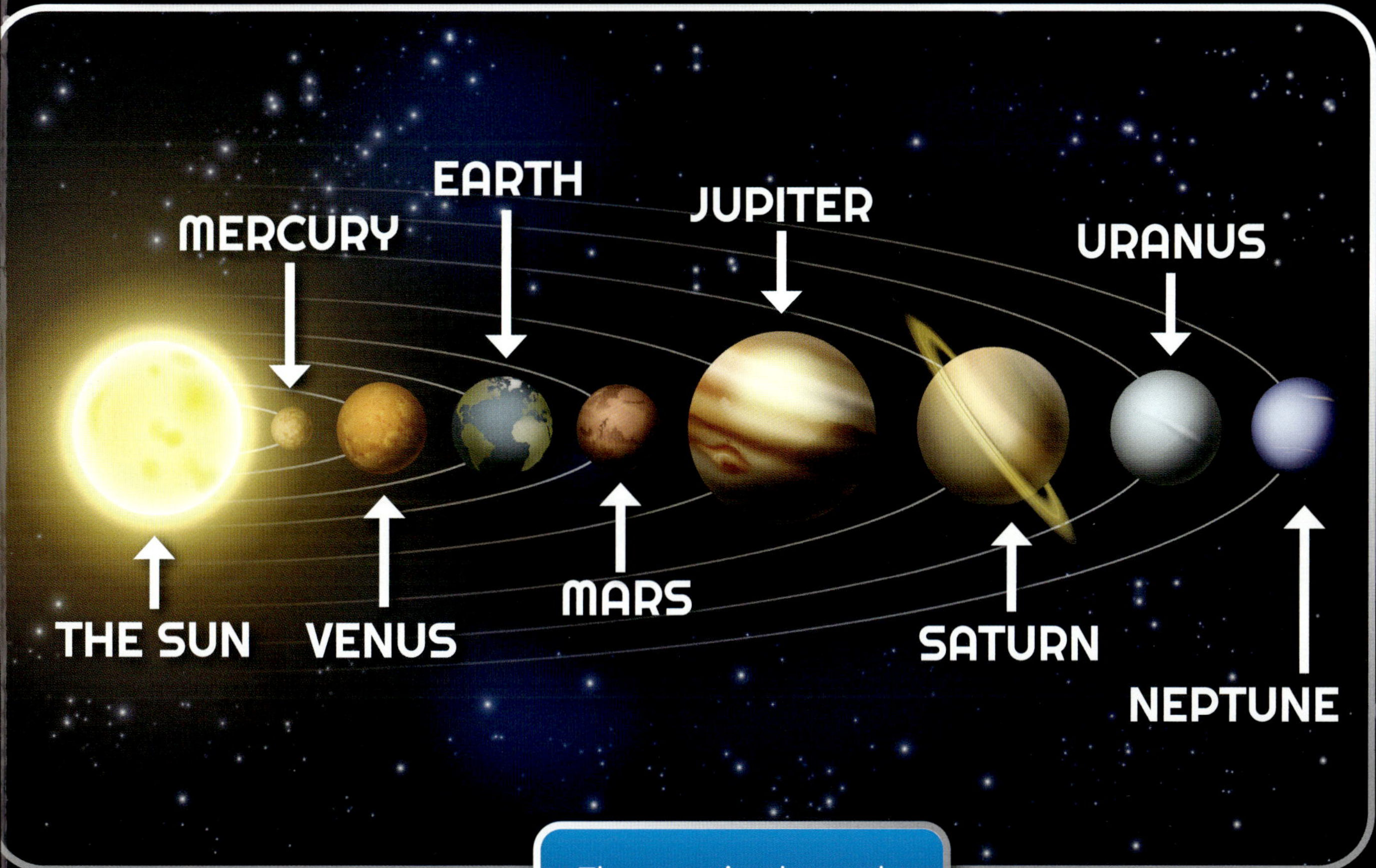

The sun is the only star in our solar system.

MERCURY

Mercury is the closest planet to the sun. However, it is only the second-hottest planet in the solar system. This is because its atmosphere is thin and does not trap much heat.

It only takes Mercury 88 days to orbit around the sun. Because Mercury orbits around the sun so quickly, it was named after an ancient Roman god who was known for his speed.

THE ROMAN GOD, MERCURY

VENUS

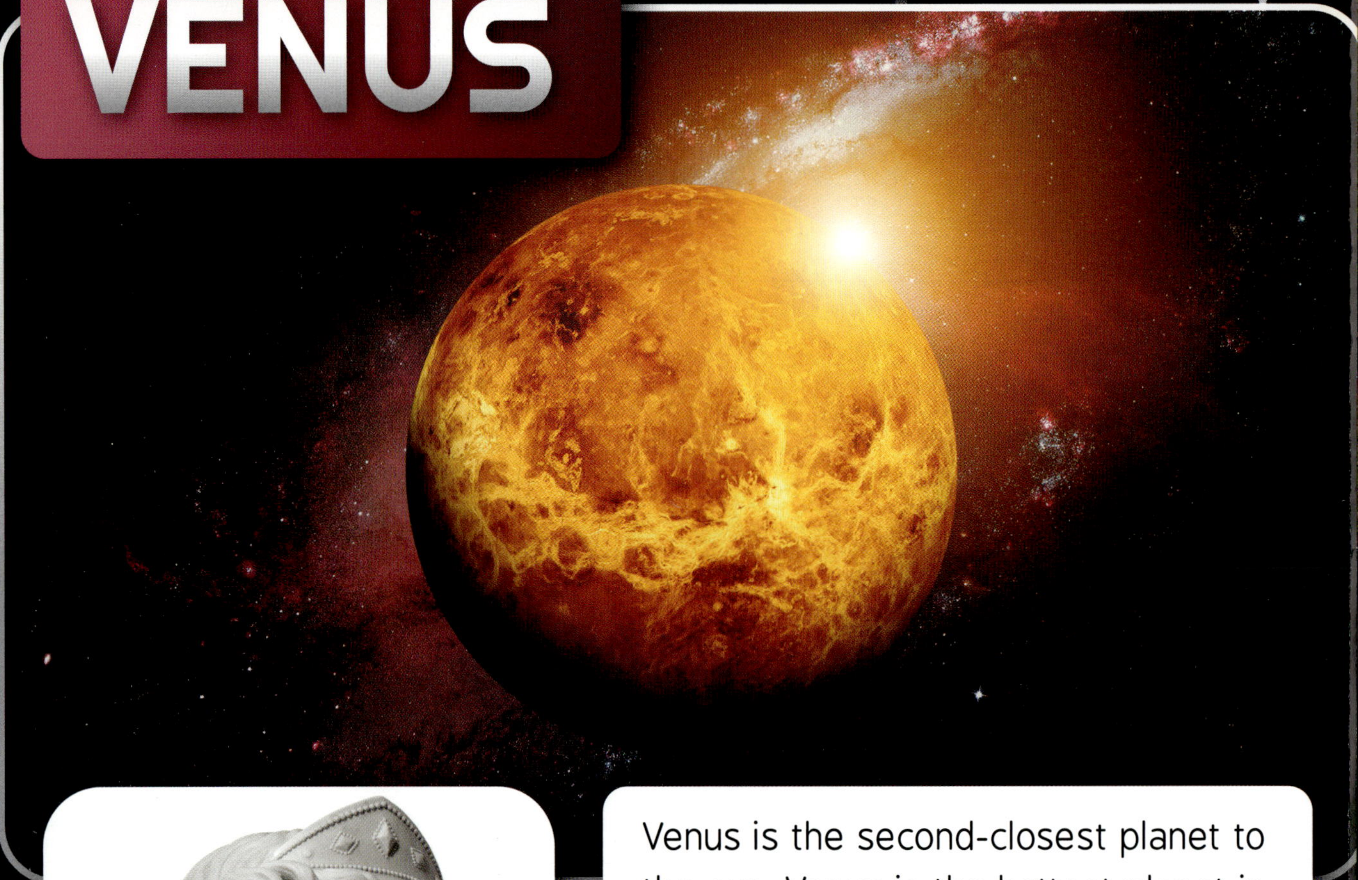

Venus is the second-closest planet to the sun. Venus is the hottest planet in the entire solar system. It is covered in a thick layer of gas that traps the heat from the sun.

VENUS

Venus is named after the ancient Roman goddess of beauty.

Venus is not much smaller than Earth. Some scientists call it Earth's twin. However, it is quite different. Venus is much too hot to live on and instead of water, it rains deadly acid.

Most places on Venus are named after important women in history and mythology.

EARTH

Earth is the third planet in the solar system. Earth is our home planet. It is where you are right now. Earth is the only planet that has life on it that scientists know of.

The word Earth means "the ground."

Some scientists call Earth "the blue planet" because it is mostly covered in water. It takes Earth around 365 days to orbit around the sun. This is how we measure one year.

Earth is over four billion years old!

MARS

Mars is the fourth planet in our solar system. Some scientists call it "the red planet." The ground on Mars is full of rusty iron, which makes the planet look red.

Iron is one of the things that makes our blood red.

There is water on Mars, but most of it is frozen. However, scientists have found dried-up rivers on Mars. This probably means there was once water flowing on Mars, like there is on Earth.

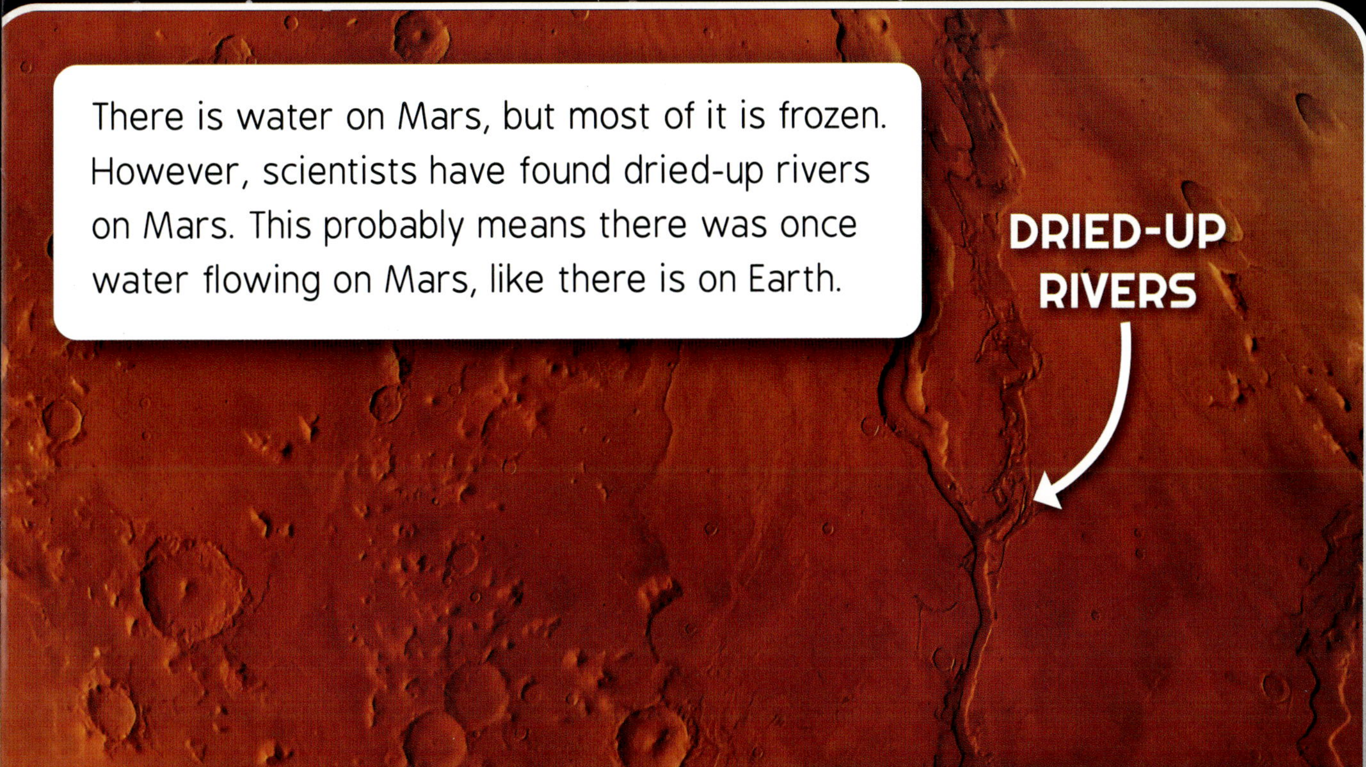

Mars was named after the ancient Roman god of war because of its blood-red color.

JUPITER

Jupiter is the fifth planet in our solar system. It is also the biggest. It is named after the ancient Roman king of the gods. The swirly patterns on Jupiter are powerful storms.

JUPITER

The Great Red Spot is a huge storm on Jupiter. Scientists believe it has been going on for over 150 years. Jupiter is made of gas and liquid. Planets like this are called gas giants.

Earth has one moon. Jupiter has 95!

SATURN

Saturn is the sixth planet in our solar system. Like Jupiter, Saturn is a gas giant. Saturn is named after the ancient Roman god of farming. The planet Saturn is famous for its rings.

SATURN

Saturn's rings are made of rock, ice, and dust. They are pulled towards Saturn by <u>gravity</u>. This is called gravitational pull. Saturn's gravitational pull causes smaller objects to orbit around it, which creates its rings.

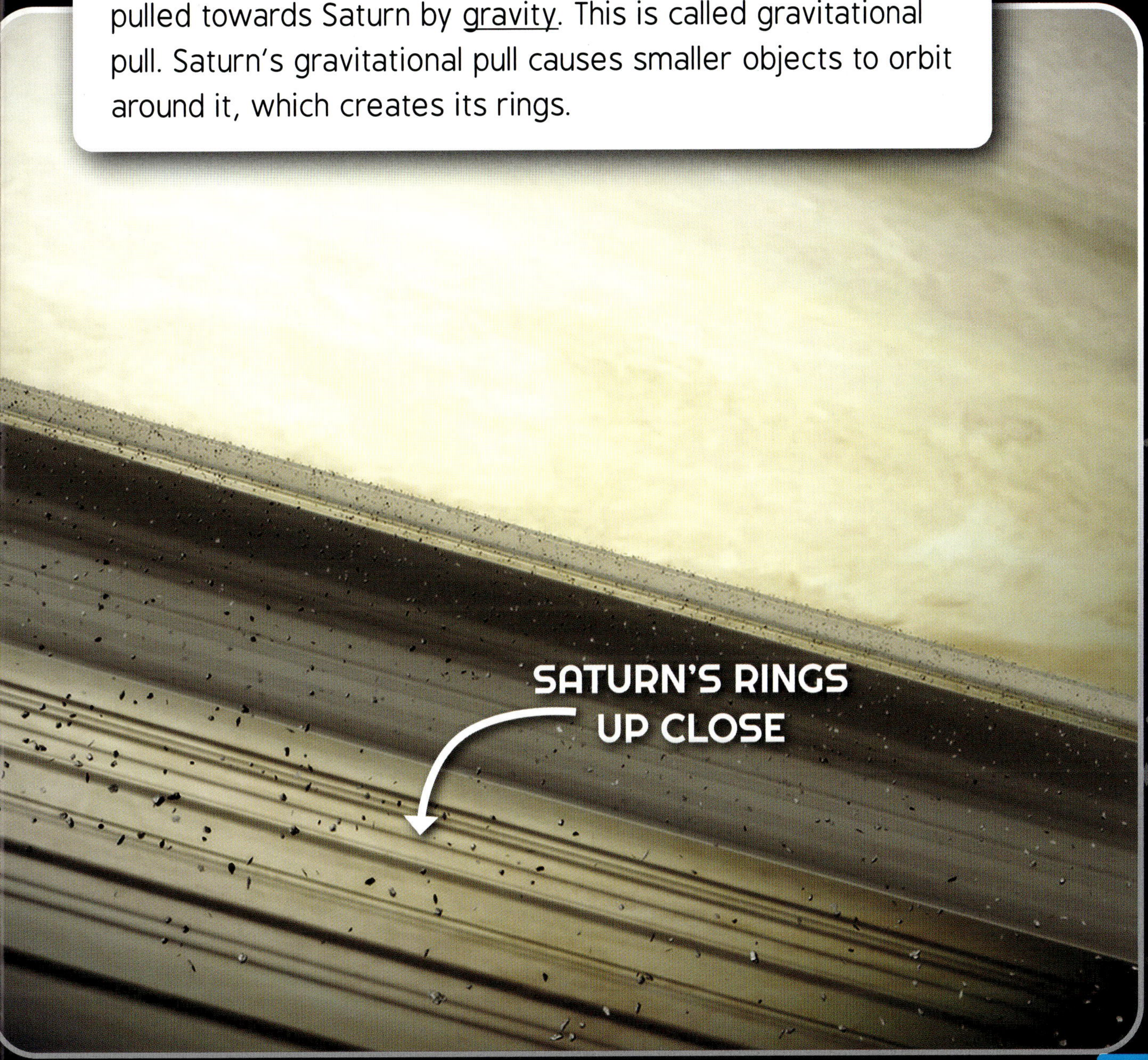

URANUS

Uranus is the seventh planet in our solar system. It is a type of planet called an ice giant. This means it is made of flowing icy materials with a frozen solid middle.

Uranus is named after the ancient Greek god of the sky.

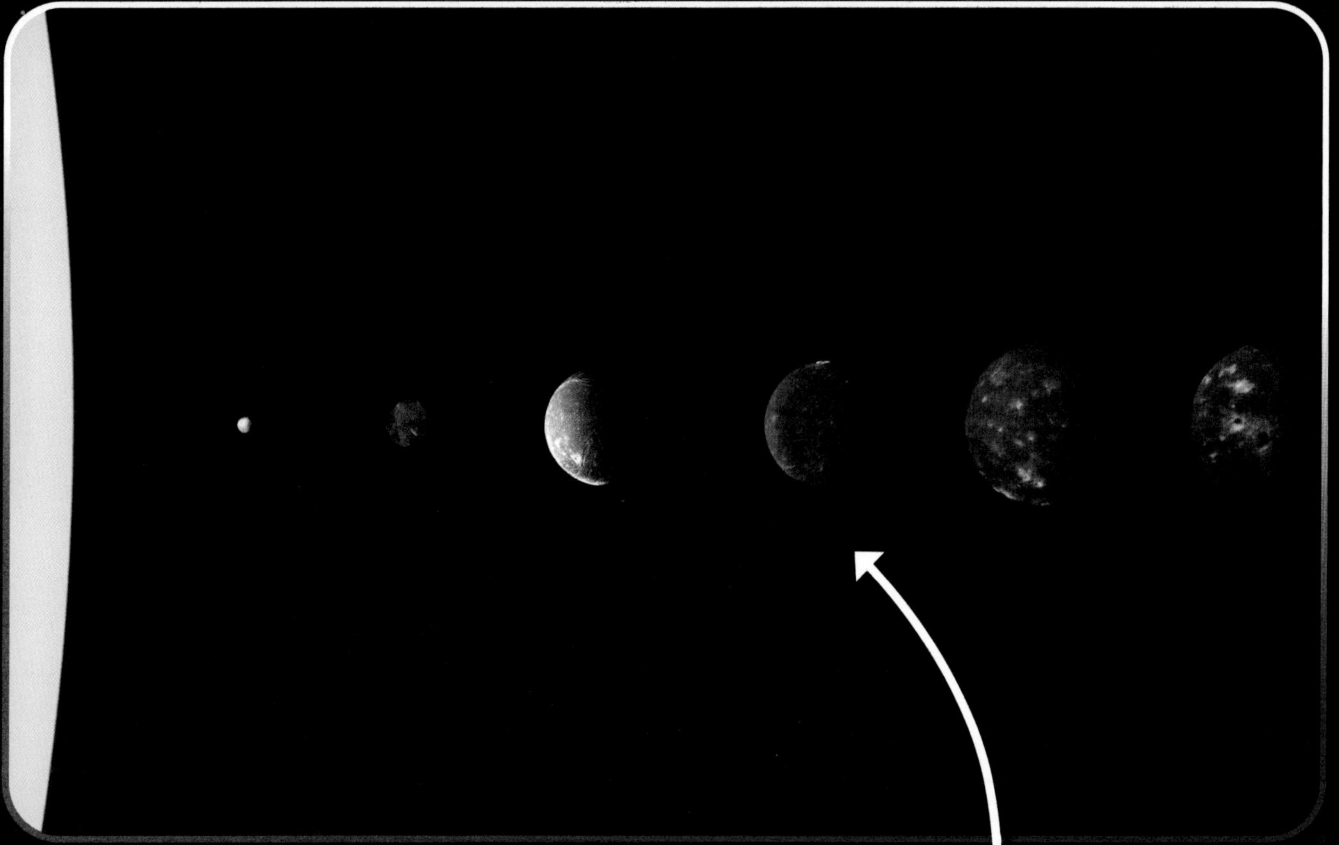

Like Saturn, Uranus is orbited by rings made of small rocks and dust that are pulled in by gravity. Uranus has 13 rings and 28 known moons. It is also the only planet that spins on its side.

NEPTUNE

Neptune is the eighth planet in the solar system and the farthest away from the sun. This means it is very dark and very cold. Neptune cannot be seen from Earth without a telescope.

Neptune has 16 moons and 6 rings made of dust that orbit around it. Like Uranus, Neptune is an ice giant. It is named after the ancient Roman god of the sea.

Every planet is different. They are all full of amazing mysteries waiting to be discovered. Which planet do you want to discover more about?

Can you remember all the planets? Try using this sentence!

My (Mercury)
Very (Venus)
Eager (Earth)
Mother (Mars)
Just (Jupiter)
Served (Saturn)
Us (Uranus)
Noodles (Neptune)

The planets are just one thing you can find in space. Space is filled with incredible things both in and outside of our solar system. Which part of space will you explore next?

GLOSSARY

acid a chemical that can break things down

ancient belonging to the very distant past

atmosphere the mixture of gases that make up the air and surround the Earth

gas a thing that is like air, which spreads out to fill any space available

gravity the force that pulls everything downwards towards the center of large objects in space

liquid a material that flows, such as water

mythology a collection of old stories that belong to a group of people

orbits repeatedly travels around an object in space

solar system a system that includes a star and everything that orbits that star, such as planets and moons

surface the outside layer of something

INDEX